*
Juniper Book 52
*

Three Books in One:

NIGHT TENNIS
by Pat Hutchings
page 3

OPEN WINDOWS
by David Bengtson
page 29

DRIVING AWAY FROM EAST TO WEST
by Karl Garson
page 61

Juniper Press
La Crosse, WI

ISBN 1-55780-110-X

Price $10.00

NIGHT TENNIS

by Pat Hutchings

Acknowledgements:

Clockwatch Review, Inside Out, Milwaukee Road Review, Northeast, and *Poetry Miscellany*

Copyright 1990 by Pat Hutchings

TABLE OF CONTENTS

FERRY PASSAGE TO MADELEINE ISLAND 5

SUNNING NAKED IN MARTHA'S BACKYARD 7

NIGHT TENNIS 8

IN A HOUSE WITH ASHTRAYS 9

CALLING HOME 10

NOTE TO MYSELF FIVE YEARS FROM TODAY 11

NOT MY FATHER, OH NO! 12

ELEGY FOR PANDA BABY, NATIONAL ZOO 13

LEARNED HELPLESSNESS 14

JACKET 15

TADPOLES 16

LONGING 17

ONE PIANO, FOUR HANDS 18

TO MY STUDENT FROM TOKYO 19

SHE CUTS HER HAIR 21

AT THIS TIME YESTERDAY 22

ON A FLUTE SOLO, MAYBE IN SATIE 23

HEMMING 24

FERRY PASSAGE TO MADELEINE ISLAND

This is the passage famous for wrecks
x'd on the map in little black.
The captain's full of facts:
depth and pressure, weight of timbers.
Here on the surface, no sign
of anything like that,
only the easy chug of the ferry
unzipping everything behind us.
It's evening
and the evening haze closes over
smaller islands near us without names.
We are moving in and out of cool holes in the air,
changes without visible source
as in a forest or a woman's body
at that time of life we do not talk about.
Again and again I come back to the moment
the sinking begins, the crew discovers
too late now: they love each other.
And I cannot cannot get out of my mind
the hundreds down, the beautiful ships,
with names remembering beautiful women,
fallen in on themselves like old men's mouths.
Not the way I want to go.
I am with a man
who would rather sleep than watch
the haze erase a hundred sails and the birds
turn in air and disappear
as if sky were skin you could get behind.
You want to feel everything,
he told me once, too much.
We are tourists, that's true, like the others
on our way to say we've been there.
And the captain is speaking
with the curious again, something about how
                                                          quickly

it comes in cold water and how whole
that same cold keeps the timbers.
Maybe there's a man down there now
in a rubber suit pawing through
St. Christophers and random change.
Crockery. I want to wake this boat up:
a bird is doing something good
with its body—aiming and then letting go, limp
and white and way up there like a handkerchief
snatched right out of a woman's hand.

SUNNING NAKED IN MARTHA'S BACKYARD

Oddly, ears are what I noticed first.
Nakedness, like blindness, blows up

sparrow rustlings in the brush
from bird to cat to large large

foot of a man who was not invited.
And notice how the body flattens

on the blue blanket, laid out like
a Simplicity pattern, all surface

turned into a giant ear. There's a nervousness
some animals are born to,

the beautiful ones, the doe
twitching at the edge of the field.

There's a nervousness
(but I mentioned that),

which is to say a nakedness
a girl learns fast is permanent:

no escaping the nosey sky,
the wind, the shower of gold

claiming to be sent by god.
So much sweet talk.

You learn to listen, or you die.

NIGHT TENNIS

Under the lights
everyone shines like a Kennedy.
They know the rules.
The darkness beyond
does not involve them,
only the expert whop, whop
of the ball whacked clean
the way it's meant to be.
This is September and
I am walking in the blackness
myself, just beyond
the light that lights up
these beautiful people like so many
Snow Whites in the crystal coffin, waiting,
whether they know it or not.
The air is like the moment
teeth hit the apple
and down by the lake
you can see the salmon slowing
down the movie, turning
soft, black.
On the nicer boulevards
all the houses are sealing themselves
like sleepers on a train moving across the great
plains
into bad weather, the kind of snow
that blanks out the picture postcard.
There are deer on the tracks.

IN A HOUSE WITH ASHTRAYS

After the party, after watching
dark forms touch and part at the curb,
mouth words, promise, nod, drive off

it is the ordinariness of each
parting I'm left with, considering
how a stranger might study

any one or two of us tonight and know
how similar are the rooms we live in
the way we go politely

back to them on a Saturday night
after drink and talk; and that
even in love, even choosing

one person out of all the others
there are many more as possible
or not. God knows

I'm nothing special myself.
My guests drive away in the watery dark.
No one's sorry. Maybe it's silence

in a house with ashtrays, that interlude
before the sparrows' clatter returns,
that makes me want to do the scene

a different way: night-shattering
shouted good-byes, kisses, dogs
in a frenzy, babies waking, porch lights

clicking on around us, the kind of
horsing around brothers do where mothers warn
somebody's going to get hurt!

CALLING HOME

My father answers and I notice again
how the voice is the last
among hair and skin and muscle
to begin to go,
his hello as constant
and as far away as Goodman
whose music used to come from his room.
And what did I read—was it yesterday—
how the child in the womb already knows
mother and father as voices
in an ambient sea?
And what did he say,
the first words muttered or blurted out
the night I was born?
On the phone I try to make my voice
cheerful, natural as a child's again;
offer something about the weather,
how sunshine here is coming
his way, out of the west
(though who can tell about the wind)
(I say that too);
how I am fine, yes, busy, yes
because that's the way we talked
at my house, never of sadness.
My father tells me he is whipping up
some noon-time casserole.
Mother is gone.
He hands the phone to my grandmother
(his mother) who no longer tries
any tricks with her voice.
I ask her about
the weather, that subject.
It has taken her
she tells me half an hour
to climb the six steps into the kitchen.
In the distance you can hear my father
fiddling with spoons.

NOTE TO MYSELF FIVE YEARS FROM TODAY

That some second destiny awaits—
we all believe, were born believing
there's a place where nothing is extraneous,
all the pieces adding up, after all, as at the end
of the play where the woman learns
the long-lost, much-loved daughter of the king
is she, herself, and the bells begin.

But this is boring. This story
stops where life kicks in.
And all that stuff about cottages
where everything will be like it was
in pastel air-brushed photographs
before you'd been there with your three valises...
So let me say this. Let me

say this: I can see you five years from today
reading this in the same room
I am writing, wearing the same
ordinary shoes and mouth. I'll wager
nothing really came of the novel.
Endings do not come to us easily.
The cat is old. The future seems to hang

before us like the indefinite weather
of Iowa that August of the blue bicycle.
Dogs circle, uneasy. Women on porches
study a place beyond the corn where sky stops
and blackness begins. Thunder ruffles
the afternoon. Where are our children?

NOT MY FATHER, OH NO!

Up on the roof
with nails in his mouth,
he begins it again: the spring
obsession with banging things back
brand new again.
His crazy rhythms drive the starlings
off the nests.

What is it you are
fixing Daddy?
I used to call up, up
through the elms.
Older now, just visiting,
my job is silence.

(I hold it like
an antique vase.)

And how many years
have I counted the strokes,
the hammering, fixing, shovelling toward
the emergency room?
I pretend to be down here
doing things that must be done
to a bed of pansies,
much too busy oh my yes
to think about bones. Oh no

not my father
way up there with the nails, the sky,
no wings on his shoulders,
and me down here
the only net.

ELEGY FOR PANDA BABY, NATIONAL ZOO

And here we go again, the old argument:
all the nurture in the world
but nature pouts, will not put out,
complains of headaches, hot weather,
TV cameras, the inflated hopes
of millions who now fall back stricken
in their armchairs. Once again
death which has undone so many
makes itself a special case.
There are close-ups in the evening news,
secretaries at the nation's water coolers
really feeling quite authentically yes
stricken. Think of the poor mother.
The vanishing species, the starving
and illiterate masses dropping like flies.
Think of the flies popping off
the northern streams on summer evenings,
a million silver new ephemera
lifting into groggy flight to mate
and fall back on the water.
It is so easy to be ironic but observe
the trout pleased as punch with the delicate husk.

LEARNED HELPLESSNESS

My friend the psychologist tells me
shocked dogs who have no levers,
no buttons, to stop the pain

simply stop trying. Yelping, howling,
all natural animal functions cease.
This is the theory

my friend calls learned helplessness.
He tells me: rats and monkeys
(rats and monkeys) have been known to flip

over on their sides, eyes clamped,
as if death would be a dream
come true. We are in the laboratory.

The dogs are getting huge
helpings of yellow nuggets
I can't help tasting.

The terrier—kid with ice cream—
goes wild with delight.
My friend says you learn not to be

attached too tight. The shock button
sits in a little black box.
At first, he says, he couldn't

touch it. Science taught him
many things are possible.
He takes me into the room with rats.

JACKET

Your jacket on a hanger on a nail
you pounded into the plaster wall
(leaving a tiny star-like mark)

even without you keeps the shape
so many winters are bound to make
more or less permanent. You

and I, let's face it, made mistakes
too bad to patch and yet with you
somewhere, elsewhere, and your coat

still here, on the nail, it's inevitable
I remember your arms. And remember
that dark road on which we wound one Fall

deep into the mountains? and the moon
lighting Rainer as if from inside
in cahoots with our oohs and aahs?

We slept that night in a darkness
pricked by stars, your breath
rising straight up in plumes

so perfectly shaped I will remember
forever though **we sometimes said nothing**
kind to each other all day that year.

TADPOLES

Eventually the squirming ones
will have their way.

You bring them home
and put them in a giant jar.
You study how the buds
still wrapped transparently in skin
will finally flower into legs.
You say their wild leaping
and thrashing at the glass
is not alarming.

Then you start imagining
how one day one will turn up
belly up beside the jar,
a jelly death.

You give them names:
Emily and Anne.

You dream about how green they'll be
and how their mouths will make adjustments
to mosquitoes;

whether the lake will be too cold

and when they'll stop reminding us
of things that never quite got born.

LONGING

After the news
after the fixing and the eating
after the business of making neat
it comes again, sometimes stealthy,

this time, freight train,
all whoosh and commotion
through the room
you thought you had straight

a painful pleasure
like seeing the ocean the first first time
seeing and knowing
the next will be a kind of subtraction

another way of saying
love is not often
presence without absence too:
the slow spring

of a branch just after
sparrows scatter.

ONE PIANO, FOUR HANDS

Eating over paper plates
cucumber sandwiches that fall
apart, we keep stuffing

the cheese back inside the bread
while the sun is probably rotting
the mayonnaise, I think

without saying. Fifty miles from any city
you throw your head back like
the fat Italian baritone:

you've got your songs. I lift the wine
out of the river, convinced again
we picked a good year.

And eventually, everything is watery
with heat, the horizon no more
definite than the dream-like

conversation we keep drifting in
and out of, the half-sleep of summer
afternoon, and the grass

sticking to our bare thighs, pricking.
In a far pasture, horses nudge against
each other in the heat, the white

one arching till I ache.
We lie on our backs thinking sun
cures all ills. In clear dry air

the blackberries burn, their thick
sugary scent bringing in a meadowful
of bees, bouncing, rubbing

furry torsoes through clover and
columbine, humming over scraps of
sandwiches we offer in bare hands.

TO MY STUDENT FROM TOKYO

Well, I've tried, Hideyo,
tried to find the words
to tell you why your words

don't sound like ours,
words for what's missing
in your strict construings.

Probably you are missing Tokyo.
You have written a poem
which you read to the class

and I take to mean you're missing
Tokyo, your mother, the house
where Kiko, best friend, must be

swelling with her pregnancy like
Sumo wrestler, watching as slowly
leg, foot, toe, earth eclipse

beneath belly and there's no more
bending even to buckle shoe.
The body is so simple.

I know there are days you hate
our grammar and our heavy food,
our giant breasts and generalizations.

I've never been to Tokyo,
but I think of you walking
down the road with Kiko, saying things

girls say, I suppose,
in every language when it comes
the time for facing up.

And I've tried, Hideyo,
tried to think of you
ten years (as we say) down the road:

You're a blur,
which may be a way of saying
forgive me: I pretended

understanding is easy; it isn't.
So much history between us.
But maybe you'll read this

ten years from now and remember
this so-hot summer in America and the night
you read your poem about home—

how all the grammar cracked wide open.

SHE CUTS HER HAIR

Right, left,
she turns her head in the double mirror.
This is the look: efficient lines
they call a frame around the face,
the kind of thing
that cares for itself.

She runs a brush around the front
tentative
up and around the ears
repeats the motion
repeats until
a rhythm sweeps her old stroke down
out into the blank
where all that dark hair used to roll
down her shoulders like a road
where anyone would love to get lost
and he loved it too
when the sun was high
to sit on the porch and gather it all
in the latest dream: a place in Spain,
a place with horses on the beaches,
braided women, loose white clothing,
sun-burned children, mandolins, so much
scattering the bathroom floor like commas.

AT THIS TIME YESTERDAY

We were (let's see) finished
shovelling and had opened
a tin of sardines
to have with bread for lunch.

Just about now we were leaning under
the kitchen table letting
the cat lick the last
oily drippings from our hands and

then you got down on your knees
and rubbed that incredible apricot
belly till the whole room hummed
electric with animal pleasure.

And it was still snowing
all this time and so we lit
the pewter hurricane lamp and burrowed into
the unmade bed, under the genuine

patchwork quilt (the stitches are splitting)
and oohed and aahed as always at how
flame keeps time with the quick music
our breathing makes. Meanwhile

the cat came like he did
the day we brought him home
and curled in the V between
your legs, and we went on and on

about that first winter together in the woods
where we learned how to live without
all this money and how to bake rye bread
and chop the wood, yes,

all about wood: what burns
and what doesn't and what is enough
to last the night, and how many

things changed when we moved to the city—
some good, some like last year.
That awful whiteness of tomorrow
also shakes me.

ON A FLUTE SOLO, MAYBE IN SATIE

So you've heard it before.
It takes you back: some wind-rippled
beige field in South Dakota
where you've never been.

In French they call it deja vu;
having no word, some borrow that.
Proust insisted a delicate taste
brings back entire an afternoon
passed with an aunt, the exact
arrangement of the parlor, flowers,
tiny cakes, cups, spoons. For Freud

the past is what you slam and lock
yourself accidently, irreversibly into
(losing a finger in the act).
But this is not like that:
Not the past of battlescars
or snapshots of a day at the beach,
but the way a flute solo, maybe in Satie,
arranges the scene and sets you
in it as if in life.

So some say memory is a machine,
some say etching into wax.
I say music: that's it: the snatch
of flute like a place you've been taken
every summer all your life and cannot find
though the maps are good and you're driving hard.
What I'm trying to say is
I dreamt of my father.
He was dancing and I knew his face
would never look that way again.

HEMMING

Because it's slow
because every stitch
is like the last

because it's last
and because it means
a kind of finish

I do it in Autumn
a good wool piece
(I will wear it next week)

laid out in my lap
a light at my shoulder.
Outside people

pass on the walk, talking
like winter will never come.
It was my mother

who taught me
this silence.

Biographical Note:

For the past three years, Pat Hutchings has lived in Washington, D.C., where she works for the American Association for Higher Education. For the previous nine years, she was a faculty member at Alverno College in Milwaukee, Wisconsin, where she taught writing, literature and interdisciplinary humanities courses.

OPEN WINDOWS

by David Bengtson

Acknowledgements:

Some of these pieces were first published in *Kabekona Journal* and *Northeast*.

The Man From Coal Lake was first published as a chapbook by Scythe Press, Dakota, Minnesota.

"On warm summer nights..." also appeared in the anthology *As Far As I Can See*, published by Windflower Press.

"What Calls Us," "'Wagon Bridge'/Philbrook, Minnesota," "Sweet Harvest," and "Japanese Garden/Little Sauk, Minnesota" were commissioned and first published by The Hart Press Inc., Long Prairie, Minnesota.

TABLE OF CONTENTS

FOR KJERSTEN, WHO IS EIGHT ... 30

WHAT CALLS US ... 32

"WAGON BRIDGE" / PHILBROOK, MINNESOTA ... 33

SWEET HARVEST ... 35

JAPANESE GARDEN / LITTLE SAUK, MINNESOTA .. 36

BLACKBIRDS ... 37

RED OAKS IN APRIL ... 39

A DRINK ... 40

THE MAN FROM COAL LAKE ... 42

FOR KJERSTEN, WHO IS EIGHT

I remember my father
lifting me to his shoulders
outside a hospital in Providence.
My grandmother, my mother's mother,
was dying in a room on the first floor.
I was too young to go inside
the hospital. So my father
carried me on his shoulders
to her window.
When he asked,
"Can you see her?"
I said, "Yes."
And I waved.

I still remember
what I saw in her window.
I saw the glare of the sun.
Squinting against the glare,
I tried to see her,
but I saw only the reflection
of my own face.

This is one lie
I cannot forget.
I don't remember
what she looked like
or where she is buried.
But I remember saying, "Yes."
And my father lowered me
to the ground.

Tonight I lift you to my shoulders
and carry you to bed.
When I bend for a kiss,
you reach out with both arms
and pull me close.
You are like a snail
stuck to an old barge.

Every night
you ask your mother
to check your heart,
assure you that it beats,
that it will beat
while you sleep.

Every night
she touches your chest.
Your heart is strong;
your shell, so thin.

And now, we watch you sleep,
your mouth open,
your breath moving slowly in
and out.

Sometimes when you breathe
so heavily,
I think that you escape
the tight body
to visit your great-grandmother.
You find her sitting
in a room of open windows.
While she tells you
of the boat and the journey,
you wind her hair into circles
on top of her head.

WHAT CALLS US

In winter, it is what calls us
from seclusion, through endless snow
to the end of a long driveway
where, we hope, it waits—
this letter, this package, this
singing of wind around an opened door.

"WAGON BRIDGE"/PHILBROOK, MINNESOTA

Wind ripples the river as it winds
around the bend and under this bridge.
Bubbles cover the surface, flickering
lights in the sun's reflection.
The banks are a thick fence
of tall canary grass.
Swarms of swallows circle from under
the bridge out over the river, swoop,
dive, weave, glide, skim the water,
swirl in constant chatter back
to their nests hidden in crosses
of worn timbers and steel.
A small yellow butterfly fights
the currents of wind to cross the river.

Most of the white pine is gone,
huge stands of pine timber torn
out before this bridge was built,
driven up the Long Prairie—sometimes
so packed that loggers could cross this
floor of bones from bank to bank—
driven into the Crow Wing
and to the Mississippi.

Years ago, on banks where trees
were left to rot, you might see children
carrying baskets, picking up pine knots
of all sizes. These knots, filled with pitch,
fueled the brilliant flames of bonfires
along the river. Sometimes at night,
the golden glow of pine knot fires
floated on the river in wire baskets
tied to the bows of fishing boats,
lighting the water and shapes of men
leaning to spear suckers. The black
smoke of pitch twists above them.

Years ago, the trip-trap of horses,
the rattle of old wagons,
the putter of the only car in Philbrook.
Beneath the bridge, children swam naked,
convinced that the water clothed them.

Years ago, while swimming across the river,
a boy from town cramped, screamed
for help, was lost to the swift current.
When the door of water closed,
he was carried to a room full of long grass
which he pulled frantically with both hands
and clenched until the door
was opened by the stiff wire
which found his body and pulled it,
grass and all, to the surface.

The river winds gently.
Under water, long strands of grass,
yellow and green, all lean north.
In the distance, the moan of an occasional
cow and the loud whistle of a train
as it nears Philbrook and
crosses the bridge down river.

SWEET HARVEST

When nights are crisp and days are warm,
the sap rises in a thousand secret wicks
to feed the flames of waiting leaves.

This is the season of sweetness.
In frosty haze we pound taps into sapwood.
The sap runs clear as water, sweet and sparkling.

With snow still thick, the first brown moths
of spring lightly flutter delicate wings
around the filling buckets.

This is the season of sweetness,
the sweet harvest of early spring.

JAPANESE GARDEN/LITTLE SAUK, MINNESOTA

In this garden one tree is weeping
while another's bent branch waits for God to sit
and the lantern rides a frozen wave.
All winter we waited for these few days
when plum and apple blossom.
Tomorrow we will walk this path again
and stand here with outstretched hands
as petals fall silent as snow.

BLACKBIRDS

        The other day a farmer told me,
        "They'll wipe out a whole field
        if you let them."

The field is
ripe with
sunflowers.

The sky,
filled with
blackbirds.

They swarm from
one field to
another, pulled
by the same thread.

Finally,
they land.

A blackbird on the bent stem
of each burned sunflower
bends to peck at the seeds.
The field now darker
than before.

Down by the lake,
three shots.
In three waves the birds fly off.
The flowers slowly nod
as the birds fill
nearby trees.

There is such
noise in those trees.

I crawl through the fence into
the field they have abandoned.
As I walk between the rows,
I can't resist touching
the fine white hair that
grows on each neck.

I can't see the birds.
Their bodies are hidden
among the bare branches
that surround this field.
But I hear them waiting
for me to leave.

At this final service
all heads are bowed.
The relatives have gathered.
They haven't spoken for years.
They argue about who will
get the large brooch.

There is such
noise in those trees.

RED OAKS IN APRIL

As
I rake,
the pile
rises to touch
the lowest
leaf.

A DRINK

When ice finally stretched across
ponds and swamp in the hollow
behind the Lutheran Cemetery
and thickened to hold even
our most tentative steps,

the hockey games began.
Every night after school,
teams were quickly chosen.
Only an hour to play
before dark.

Between hunks of wood
marking the goals at each end
stood the two worst players.
Someone always brought a puck
with initials carved
carefully and deep.

Then the call,
"We'll bring it up,"
as the best skater on that team
cradled puck against black blade
and began the races
to the other end.

The clatter of sticks,
the slash of blades into ice
echoed across the hollows,
rose to the cemetery
where even in winter
young couples walked and kissed—

where, in summer, they made love
hidden by tall grass, bouquets of dead flowers,
and scores of scarred slate gravestones—
where we, once, hiding flat
on the roof of the custodian's shack,
watched wide-eyed and quiet.

At the end of the game
when puck became shadow,
we hammered the butt ends of our sticks
through the ice to make
holes big enough for a drink.

At any other time of year
we thought it crazy to drink
swamp water with its green
screen of scum and bugs.
Only rocks, sticks, a turtle or snake
broke that opaque surface.

But in winter, weary after the sweat of hockey,
we stretched out on our pocked pond
and in the grey light
sipped from this muddy bowl
the most delicious dark water of all.

II
THE MAN FROM COAL LAKE

On warm summer nights he walks to the silo to sing. While the barn slowly sinks into itself, the silo is tall and strong and still the perfect place to sing.

He brings white candles and some matches and climbs into the silo, empty now since most of the cows were sold. He lights a candle, pushes it into the packed silage, and begins to sing quietly.

The sounds of old hymns ascend to the roof of the silo. Sounds that soar forty feet into the air and return to surround him like the pines deep inside the woods. There is no sound like the sound of a silo singing.

His voice carries outside to the hills, into the woods, across the lake, where it joins with the sound of the bared roots of old oaks, the sound of corn squeaking in the garden, the sound of two sorrel mares standing close, the sound of pine needles dropping, the sound of jumping fish.

On a night like this he brings a good supply of candles.

Out in a hollow between two hills two horses graze. Two old sorrel mares with Norwegian names. Sometimes on summer days when the heat is thick, he puts a handful of oats into his pocket and walks out to the horses. As he walks, he keeps track of dead trees and fallen limbs for firewood.

The path takes him past an overturned boat, once green, the center board warped and falling into the open bottom. Past old fence lines that disappear in the underbrush. Past the stone foundation of the old Steinert place, now filled with dead limbs, cement chunks, rotting boards, and a rusted bucket. Two vine-covered ironwood trees persist in this debris. Nearby an old oak has been ripped from the ground by a violent wind, the roots washed bone-clean by the rain.

He sits for a moment on one of the foundation stones, a stone too big for one man to carry. The smell of spearmint is all around him.

With his anchor pulled into the boat, he lies back with his head on the bow seat and lets his hands touch the water. He loves to feel the water with his fingers, and he does not go home when it starts to rain.

The boat begins to fill with water and small fish the size of raindrops. Fish eggs from another lake, caught up into the clouds and hatched, now fall into this lake, into this boat.

When the sun returns, he lifts a handful of fish close to his eyes and sees the lines of his hand through their delicate bodies.

Today his black Lab leads him between the barn and the granary and out to the woods. With each step grasshoppers flit into the air—five, six at a time—flying in all directions. Two crows circle overhead and drop into the tops of two adjacent pine trees, heaving their weight from side to side.

The dog heads down the path, then ignores it and bellies under an old wire fence to follow a scent in a different direction. Sometimes a scent takes him to the other side of the lake. Days later, his black head bobs in the water as he returns, tired and slightly smaller.

So he walks to the lake, not thinking of the path or the thistles that catch on his pants but of the hook slowly sinking to the bottom. Suddenly he stops and begins to measure the line against the length of his own body, pulling the string up from the ground and tying knots in front of his eyes. Later, when he drops the line into the water, the knots will rub between his thumb and finger, and he will know how deep the hook descends.

He winds the string around the stick. There is something heavy on the end of the line. Heavier than a fish and without a struggle—a dead weight. No need to wind fast. Up into the boat he pulls a burlap sack, a piece of twine knotted tight around the open end. When he drops the bag onto the floor of the boat, there is a thud, a muffled sound.

No need to open the sack. He lowers it into the water, and when the weight is gone, he breaks the line and reaches for another hook.

As soon as the ice is a few inches thick, they start to move their fish houses onto the lake. All winter long they move their houses. From one side to the other, from one lake to another. Those that stay in one place sink deeper and deeper into the ice.

He has never used a fish house. They say it's because he doesn't want anyone to know where the good fishing is. He says the shadow of the house keeps the fish away.

Two or three times a week, in early morning, he crosses the ice to the marsh on the east side of the lake to check the muskrat traps. In the distance the dark mounds of mud and reeds rise two, three feet above the ice. Behind them, the outline of the hills.

The ice thunders beneath his feet. He stops, thinks of a fox along the edge of the marsh feeding on the haunches of a large deer carcass. All around him, the reeds arch like jumping fish, only to be caught twice by the ice.

Above him, the sky opens with the first signs of sunlight. He walks to the mounds, removes all of the traps, and then heads for home. His feet press into clean crusted snow and the muskrat traps slap against his legs.

When he goes ice fishing, he brings an ice pick, a piece of twine, and a hook. He walks to the middle of the lake, kneels, chops a hole in the ice, and drops his line and hook into the water. When his coat pockets are full of crappies, he puts his line and hook inside his mitten and walks home. He empties his pockets onto the kitchen counter and turns to warm his hands over the oil burner.

Behind him, the crappies begin to move, and one flops onto the floor. Soon all of the fish are on the floor and flopping against the door. So he opens the door and follows them back to the middle of the lake. He chops a hole in the ice and helps each one back into the water. And then he waits until the hole is closed.

Sometimes in early spring when the ice is breaking up on the lake, his cows stray out for a drink. While they are on the ice, large chunks begin to break loose and drift away. Today all eight of his cows are floating in the middle of the lake. Eight black and white cows, each on her own white island, mooing. So he puts his boat into the dark water, rows out to them, and with a long piece of rope pulls each cow back to shore.

The black dog has been gone for weeks now. Disappeared. He always came back from the other side of the lake. Not this time.

The man walks for miles on gravel roads, his eyes straining, jaw set tight, hands stuffed into his overalls, hoping to see the black body ahead. An accident he could accept. Even dead is better than not at all.

He thinks—not much of a watchdog. Always came when anyone called...

"Here boy. C'mere boy." The back door slams shut and the car screeches toward blacktop two miles away, a beer bottle tossed out into the dust.

Still, sometimes at dusk while standing on the back steps, he sees the black head bobbing in the water and runs down to the lake. Only a wave or a turtle shell, a piece of driftwood. The head of a dog that belongs to the lake.

The horses don't run away when they see him. They know about the oats. As the older one nuzzles into his overall pocket, he strokes her neck, holds her long, tangled mane and throws himself up onto her back.

She walks slowly to the lake. At the edge she splashes the water with her hoof. When she is too deep to stand, he wraps both arms around her neck and lies flat out on her back. Somehow her heavy body stays afloat. Her old muscles stretch and tighten as she paws the water with thin legs not made for swimming. Her back is smooth and slippery. Her tail fans out behind her. As she swims, the old body is renewed.

She is a wild-eyed, young mare galloping in a hollow between two hills, racing to the top where she stops and strikes the rocky ground with her hoof. The sun is high. She comes to the edge of a lake and takes the first drink.

The other mare has followed them to the lake and waits. She calls to the horse in the lake, who answers and turns back to shore. In the shallow water he slides off her back and heads for home. His clothes will dry quickly in this heat.

Tonight he cannot sleep. Down at the lake the fish are jumping. He dresses quickly and leaves the house without even knotting the laces of his boots. In the distance the lake is alive with light. Fish rise, drawn up by the moon, then arch back into the water. Above the lake are thousands of shining fish. Each eye and scale absorbs the light. Even the bait fish close to shore know the secret of jumping at night. And at the end of each short flight the fish push circles of water toward the shore.

So he watches from the edge of the lake. He has been here before when the fish jump at night. He steps out of his boots and into the water, letting the waves wash up to the middle of his calves. Delighted by the performance and standing now waist-deep in water, he begins to applaud.

Biographical note:

David Bengtson grew up in Cranston, Rhode Island. He graduated from Concordia College in Moorhead, Minnesota, and received an M.A. in English from the University of Minnesota. He lives with his wife, Marilyn, and daughters, Cory and Kjersten, in Long Prairie, Minnesota, where he teaches high school English.

DRIVING AWAY FROM EAST AND WEST

by Karl Garson

Acknowledgements:

Cimarron Review, Northeast, South Dakota Review, Cream City Review, Kansas Quarterly, and *The Ohio Journal.*

Copyright 1990 by Karl Garson

TABLE OF CONTENTS

AT SUNSET LAKE 65

AUGUST, SELWAY-BITTERROOT WILDERNESS 66

APRIL SNOW IN WISCONSIN 67

SEARCH FOR A NEW CALF 72

THE RETURN 73

DRIVING IOWA 1 74

OCTOBER REFLECTION 75

WINTER CAMP, THE NORTHERN HIGHLANDS 76

MANET DECORATES MITCHELL 77

MORNING FLIGHT 78

SOUTHERN WIND 79

HEMLOCKS 80

IOWA, FROM MONTANA 81

DOE AT 6AM 82

FIFTH AUTUMN IN BOISE 83

BONE LAKE, CHRISTMAS '80 84

AN AFTERNOON OF FOWLES ABANDONED 85

AT SUNSET LAKE
    for Mary Shumway

The gusts and cold again to this moraine
and to the lake below where shards
of ice grip blue-lit reeds
shaken out of summer.

Here I argue mood
in autumn shapes like weather
torn from null, uncertain as wind
whether it will ridge or trough.

AUGUST, SELWAY-BITTERROOT WILDERNESS

At the outlet, a few feet above a small dam
that doglegs Bass Lake back to Bass Peak,
I stop in slack weather.

Here no wind, no riffle. 2,000 feet up, a ridge
runs south to the peak, shows wind will build,
will strop 500 feet from brushline to crest
                                            tombstone smooth.

An hour's rest. After, I climb northwest to a saddle,
a small meadow notched in the ridge. I set camp,
shock cord the tent, then switch down a
                                            cirque for water,

spot beer a packer stashed, cool some in the pond
then lie sunning on a rock. Aspen upslope
quiet at the talus edge.

The beer helps me climb back. With dark, a
                                            quarter moon glints
the ridge south. My fire flicks dull claws
                                            at the universe.
I can't sleep, yet I dream wind.

APRIL SNOW IN WISCONSIN

I

That year spring turns on the winter and wins,
but snow returns so thick in wind
that plow clicks in my mind like a stutter
while I look two ways at the order of the farm.

The day becomes a trip postponed and a barn
                                            to clean.
Measured by accumulations
it tosses on the swell of weather.
The roads close. A neighbor phones for help.

A minute later, his, "Come quick, the calves
                                          are dying,"
would have waited
while the manure and its stale steam
spread over the lower forty.

But the load waits instead. It won't freeze
in weather this wet. I snap the M tractor free
for a trip through a wood that marks
good neighbors with maple and oak.

II

Not a track in the wood shows life. None of
                                          the deer
or squirrel. Most everything waits this one out.
As the tractor breaks trail toward the Webers,
a single jay blues the air.

The lane skirts a kettle of rough hay. In bow season
last fall Joe Weber hit a buck here
and called for help tracking. We followed blood
two hundred yards north. Above a ravine we lost it.

It was almost dark and our lanterns weren't sun.
Joe tied his scarf to a branch. "He broke
off the shaft, probably. The wound closes
and the blood flows in. I'll come back tomorrow."

That day, Saturday, I got my limit of squirrel
and walked to the Webers for a snack.
Margaret Weber made the best orange cookies
in Caledonia township. Joe was in the kitchen
                                              eating some.

"No luck," he said. "Since you had the oak logged
off that slope the ravine has gone thick in berries.
If he got in there to die only the fox will know,
and do by now, probably." I took a cookie.
                                      Margaret poured coffee.

Joe's Uncle Cliff came in from the barn.
His Angus cows were calving. "Wish I could be lazy,
hunting like you two." He washed, then grabbed
                                                a cookie.
Joe took another. I got the last. Margaret laughed at
                                                    Cliff.

III

That winter, putting up wood, I worked up
                              some oak tops
the logging crew left along the ravine.
And ten feet of hollow heart trunk
not good enough for lumber but good enough
                                        for heat.

I cut the trunk into sections from the top
then flipped it with a peavey.
But in the snow I read the slope wrong.
The thing rolled till the berry vines caught it.

I slid down with a log chain, backed up
the tractor, and pulled it out. Lucky.
But down there the ribs of Joe's buck
                              showed through.
I found the arrow and all. Fox had filled
                                   on the rest.

An ax got the skull and antlers.
Next night when I went to the Webers for
                              some euchre
I brought it along. Joe took it.
In the dark he nailed it to the side of Cliff's barn.

IV

You think of these things, nothing else to do
with a mile of wet snow piling up
and a neighbor needing help. Then, out of the trees
and there's Cliff wringing his hands, waiting. "Glad
                                          you're here."

We run to the first three. They lie flat in the
                                      lee of the barn,
under Joe's trophy. You don't look twice at
                                      a calf's eyes
when they're like that. You know. "There are
                                    more in the barn,"
Cliff says, "I'll run call the vet again."
                                              He's gone.

Of the four in the barn three are gone.
I lean low to the other in the wet matted straw
to listen for breath, for any thin gift,
some oddment to offer Cliff.

There's a last breath, then nothing.
Angry, I yell, "No you can't! No you can't!"
But the small form won't startle. The spine arches
away from me and all surprise.

Cliff's back. "The vet's stuck at Blystone's. Ed's
going to try to get him here with the wrecker."
"Well Cliff, I think we're stuck here too."
I grab his shoulder and wait him out.

V

We drag the four into the yard
and catch sight of Ed's wrecker rattling
                                            in on chains.
"Poison," from the vet.
The four of us look for a source.

We find a scrapped door over the stock tank.
"Threw it over this morning to keep out the snow.
Wanted to keep it from slushing up."
The thick coats of leaded, white paint are
                                              chewed away.

That's all we need to see. Ed takes off with the vet.
Cliff and I go inside for coffee and cookies.
"They're pretty small. I'll drag 'em to the
                                              woods Cliff."
"More fox than usual this year anyhow."

"Someone has to smile," Margaret says.
Cliff and I get rid of the door and drain the tank.
We get it scrubbed and filled. He lets some
                                              penned stock out
after we drag the seven from the yard.

One by one, snapped to the end of the chain, I skid
them through wet and deepening April snow.
Six cups and cookies between the trips.
Then in dark I retrace the lane toward chores.

I see each trip.
The snow steams off the exhaust. The chain slacks
                                              and snaps.
A strange cortege: the M tractor and I and each calf,
thumping to the ravine of fox and seasoned oak.

SEARCH FOR A NEW CALF

Over hay stubble a night bird skims
and dips, a Wisconsin flying fish
my eyes follow into starless dark,

into rough pasture crooked by rising water
where peepers call, where fireflies point
the fresh mist as I search for a new calf,

while the hills west stoke thermals
that can flash and smother new life
caught in its sleep by their sudden crest.

All afternoon the cow stayed in brush here,
kept close to the river with her thirst
and still as the night is still now.

But tonight the riverbank brush is empty.
And the path from there, a half-circle
hammered upstream, ends in a flooded slough.

I criss-cross the higher ground, move
hunch by hunch and wobble a light
into place after possible place.

When I finally find them safe,
sheltered and warmed by cairned stone,
cleared years back from the hayfield,

the west has gentled into stars that lead
my walk home, while behind me the Baraboo
drops and bends for the Wisconsin.

THE RETURN

Redwing measures
note the point of Aries.

Acres loose another frost
again to house spring's immigrant.
What they cannot absorb
ponds around the cattails.

I leave the cabin.
My young spaniel leagues ahead.

This eighty
a fresh washed cupboard.
Our steps
the dishes back in.

DRIVING IOWA 1

Sirius dances the gunmetal sky
with an eighth grown from the new moon
and Linn County hills along Iowa 1
sequin like the bodice of a party dress
on the pipe rack of a secondhand.

Nights with this look, close to the thick bone
of winter, all that keeps anyone quick
is a Purex box or such, flat against their grille.
If the hot light blinks red they stop,
tear some away, then keep rolling.

January '82, a Friday late and cold
as stone at a felon's head,
wind under light this thin ripped
ground cover snow into blizzard.
In a half hour almost everyone hit the ditches.

If they stayed on the road they stuck it out too,
till plows and Saturday sun took some drifts down.
The county crews found heifers and a farm
                                       dog frozen to fences.
And ten feet from their belly-up Dodge, the
                                               Hackett kids
stood against brush, still holding hands like life.

OCTOBER REFLECTION

Of African mahogany, the fine escritoire glows
chestnut in a sudden and ample afternoon light
that slants into a day bedded late in October.

The motes are strung thin along saffron shafts.

Somewhere, perhaps two clean rooms off, a
refrigerator tends a selection of fine food
kept to hand for eventual whim.

The andirons cradle white oak seasoned
                                      to leap blue.

East, at the marsh, sedge at its rim
browns in the wind, chills, and the almond
shaped leaves litter the red-veined brush.

The greens give up to a ghost blown south.

And the smaller fowl with the geese beat
east, and all life born to air pins to a water's edge
somewhere below, another night's hope.

Their gabble rings on obsidian air.

West, a chandelier suns the damask, the tabled
crystal, and the gabble turned to feast
with its back to the dark.

The marsh sleep dreams of a warm sun south.

In the walls, a patient sun burns from cradled oak.

WINTER CAMP, THE NORTHERN HIGHLANDS

We stamp out a tent bed
in spent light.
Spend the night headed north.

The deadmen hold steady,
three to the wind,
one to the lee.

And the tent, taut to begin,
shudders and quiets
to looseness at dawn.

I start the brass stove,
a shriek that breaks still air
and heat that's quick with water.

After chocolate,
I sugar oatmeal
and pour black tea.

You stir from your warm night,
nose like a chuck
from your blue mummy bag.

Later, as we wax skis, pack
for the ridge;
a moraine and its lake where

in summer, after loons,
we slept to frogs,
the pulse now frozen below us;

I roll our tent,
force from it trapped air,
all trace and echo of our sharing.

MANET DECORATES MITCHELL

Forgive me,
but when you
(red hair)
greeted me, finally home
as you were
(rust coat - black hat and scarf)
from work, when
we held the moment, corralled
on the
(blue and cream spread)
bed, before the souffle
(cheese, perfectly golden and risen)
needed you too,

I meant to say,
you shot through
the slack
(wan, wood-smoked whey)
afternoon like
Manet's Olympia would
crimson
a mother superior's chapel
in any
Mitchell, South Dakota.

MORNING FLIGHT

A short pause from hot cup sees them by,
the rock doves that are swift to the mill,

where they whirl over points of spilt grain,
then descend, the first streaks of the dawn.

SOUTHERN WIND

We trade sleep for beers.

Then I drive late rain
while a scrap of you
scratches my mind.

Deer leap the grille.

The blacktop is a wake of skids.
If anything kills me
it will be the way you hold me now.

HEMLOCKS

The still inlet
floating stars
on our return
to Back Bay,

perhaps
hemlocks
somber runners
lacy over hills
to the channel,

or

esses
of hair
of firelight
circling your face,

make the recall of October
available in focus
on the occasions
corporal or spiritual
when we brush.

IOWA, FROM MONTANA

An afternoon which offers the possibility
of nothing begins to rain.
Outside the window a plum tree
declines from bloom.
The fruits of summer are a thin belief.

Maybe it is sunny in Coralville,
your Iowa town with its Florida name.
Perhaps the oaks on the library hill
gather shadows like sticks
thrown to a table in a children's game.

Here a Salt Creek truck passes
                    TRAVEL BIG WYOMING
in tall red letters to my desert room.
I feel a Wyoming highway, that stretch below Teton,
187, Pinedale to Rock Springs where
a wave for help could flap in your rear-view forever.

But the incoming rain becomes harder
and the petals fall under fire.
I go back to the refrigerator
determined to salvage
the remains of afternoon light.

Now a train grinds rust from the lumberyard siding,
like this, the smaller metal sound of a tab
pulled to open the last beer,
to signal that one things leads from another,
that with you there I've begun to drink more here.

DOE AT 6AM

Dropping from McClure Pass
at steady speed in new light toward Paonia
I see her, sacked potatoes at a half mile,
at a quarter, casualty.

Flat in my lane and still living
she tries one more leap
then settles, heaving and eyes open,
to the center line.

Her pulse arrests me and I stop,
search the Kelty till I find it, get out
to trace the rimrock east and west
and watch scared breath in chill air.

I trouble and stall, study sage,
judge she'll take time dying,
then slice hard and deep toward her spine.
She jerks like a banjo. I hug her for us both.

I soak the shirt in motel sinks
but the spot stays,
and the way sun lit the valley
as I dragged her into brush.

FIFTH AUTUMN IN BOISE

No easy task
resisting
the season's cue
to gloom.
After all
it has all those
leaves
going for it,
all that death rendered
in yellow and brown.

Nonetheless, I tell
myself
this year's been good,
has borne with it
rewards.
The pay raise is
important.
Yes, I tell myself
it is.

During walks
why then do leaves
litter as they
wither at my feet
into patterns
of a life.

BONE LAKE, CHRISTMAS '80

The wind finally slack, we pole our way
between saffron hummocks, then edge Bone Lake
over bay ice so thick it will sail into April.

The far shore rises clean and spruce
are thick along it. To our right the
lake widens, marked by a bare crop of stone.

What progress we make in stillness.
Among the dense green trees the brass stove
is quickly lit, water boils, the coffee warms us.

Our cups in hand, we ski slow to the headland.
The sun is direct and warm. A fisherman squats
                                                     on the ice.
A black dog jumps and a red mittened child
                                                     pulls a sled.

On the way back to St. Paul we laugh—
how the Labrador barked at the
                                           wound-down perch—
and we bet our promise against the slumping sun.

In this story's tomorrow you drive on south.
And I fly west reminded of coffee,
of life bright before me and the space
                                               between us dead.

AN AFTERNOON OF FOWLES ABANDONED

With your sure step and quiet way white
                                            wine arrives,
and Jonathans sliced
and cheddar cubed, on a plate like the wine
                                            glass, chilled.

The moment with the french doors you
                                            opened, closes.
A late slant of sun breaks beneath scud, scatters
gold in the cheap wine, makes it better
                                            than expensive.

I snack, sip, and the room smacks of your
                                            rust sweater,
of your navy skirt,
of your knee socks and light blue panties
                                            and bra and

I open the french doors and walk to where you curl
                                            studying Fowles.
I bury my face in your corduroy lap, tell you
                                            gold jug wine
and cheddar cubed and Jonathans sliced are the
                                            finest of poems.

We move to the spirit of your verse. The French
                                            Lieutenant's Woman,
a shallow tent pitched,
on the still warm cushion of your chair.

Biographical Note:

A Wisconsin native, Karl Garson graduated from Marquette University, flew for the U.S. Navy in Vietnam, and studied with Richard Hugo at the University of Montana. He received his MFA from Montana in 1981.

His poetry has appeared in *Blue Unicorn, Cimarron Review, Cream City Review, Gryphon, The Kansas Quarterly, Northeast, The Ohio Journal, Poetry Now, The Reaper, South Coast Poetry Journal,* and *South Dakota Review,* among others. His first book of poetry, *Thoughts in Available Light,* was published by Song Press in 1982.

Karl taught writing for 14 years at the University of Wisconsin— Stevens Point, Boise State University, and the University of Arizona. In 1989 he accepted an editorial position with the *Daily Racing Form* in Hightstown, New Jersey.

His Turf writing includes news and feature articles in the *Daily Racing Form, The Florida Horse, Racing Action, QuarterWeek, Thoroughbred Times,* and - *Western Racing News.*

Karl lives in Howell Township, New Jersey, with his wife, Margaret Hendershot.

NORMANDALE COMMUNITY COLLEGE
LIBRARY
9700 FRANCE AVENUE SOUTH
BLOOMINGTON, MN 55431-4399